REACHING FOR THE STARS

JULIA ROBERTS

Prettiest Woman

by Rosemary Wallner

Published by Abdo & Daughters, 6535 Cecilia Circle, Edina, Minnesota 55439.

Library bound edition distributed by Rockbottom Books, Pentagon Tower, P.O. Box 36036, Minneapolis, MN 55435.

Library of Congress Number: 91-073038 ISBN: 1-56239-055-4

Cover photo: Retna Ltd.
Inside photos: Retna Ltd.: 4, 11, 17, 25, 27, 29, 31; Fotos International: 7, 19; Pictorial Parade: 22

Edited by Bob Italia

TABLE OF CONTENTS

A RISING HOLLYWOOD STAR

"I think I'm loud and weird," said Julia Roberts when asked to describe herself in a 1989 interview. It's true that many people have found her outgoing, outspoken, larger than life, and a little kooky. But her costars have called her "genuine," "good and kind," and "amazing and incredible."

Just a few years after leaving her hometown in rural Georgia, Julia Roberts is now the fastest-rising star in Hollywood. She can reportedly ask for–and get–one million dollars for a movie appearance.

Her good looks have put her on two most-beautiful-women-in-the-world lists and on many magazine covers. Roberts, however, has said she rarely wears makeup because she doesn't like to call attention to her mouth, which she says is too big.

"When she enters a room," said the screenwriter for one of her films, "it's like somebody just turned up the lights. And it gets a little dimmer when she leaves."

In just a few years, Julia Roberts has worked to make her film career grow from small movie parts to larger starring roles.

"She's an original, in a category all to herself," said one director, "which probably helps to explain how she's captured everyone's attention so quickly."

From a slow start as a model to a nationally known actor, Julia Roberts has come a long way. As she continues to accept more and more roles, her fans can expect more great things from this talented Georgia native.

LIFE IN SMYRNA, GEORGIA

Julie Roberts was born in 1967 in Smyrna, Georgia, a small town northwest of Atlanta. Her parents, Walter and Betty Roberts, already had two children–Eric, who is eleven years older than Julie, and Lisa, who is two years older.

Roberts's parents owned and operated the Roberts's Theatre Workshop. They taught young actors all about the theater and put on plays for the local community. Although the workshop never made much money, Roberts's parents were happy to be working with creative and talented people.

As she was growing up, Julia wanted to be a veterinarian; but a career in acting was always at the back of her mind.

"[The workshop's] purpose had nothing to do with money or recognition," explained Roberts, "it was about acting, performing." Some of Roberts's earliest memories are of "just being a little kid and watching [my parents] do plays in the park."

The workshop closed, however, when Roberts was four years old. That year her parents divorced and her father and brother moved to Atlanta. Julie and Lisa stayed with their mother in Smyrna.

As a young girl, Roberts took care of the family's many animals and dreamed about becoming a veterinarian. But acting was also a strong interest. "It was just kind of there in my mind all the time," said Roberts.

When she was nine years old, Roberts's father died. The shock of losing a parent was hard on her. "I had a great relationship with my dad," Roberts recalled. "Nothing intellectual, just really caring and fun. I miss my dad." The rest of her family remained close and supported each other.

"I come from a real touchy family," said Roberts. "A lotta hugging, a lotta kissing, a lotta love."

In school, Roberts was more interested in writing and reading than in working on math problems.

During one of her English classes at Campbell High School, the teacher showed an old movie. Roberts fell in love with the movie and again began to think about an acting career. But she kept at her writing.

"The school had a handful of really great teachers," said Roberts, "and I started getting more and more interested in writing, with some encouragement."

Most of the time Roberts was just like everyone else. "I wasn't great at anything," recalled Roberts, "just a middle of the road, basic kid."

Because she was outgoing, Roberts made many friends. "You want to really know what I remember about Julie?" said one friend. "She had this incredible hyena-like laugh. The whole class would have to stop to let her get it out of her system."

Another friend remembered Julie's early acting attempts. "When we got bored," said her friend, "Jules could be real creative. She could muster up tears in a second to get out of homeroom, and I'd have to follow her out to help her."

By the time she was a senior in high school, Roberts had decided what she wanted to do with her life. She wanted to act. And the best place to learn how was in New York City.

AUDITIONING, WAITING, ACTING

Three days after graduating from high school, Roberts went to New York City to study acting and live with her sister. Lisa also wanted to be an actor, and Roberts looked to her for guidance and protection.

"Lisa really cushioned a lot of things for me," said Roberts. "I always considered her fearless. When we were kids, I always thought she would protect me. And at seventeen in New York, it was the same thing."

One of the first things Roberts did in New York was register her name in the Screen Actors Guild. When she did, she found that there already was an actor with the name Julie Roberts. That's when she decided to change her name to Julia Roberts.

For a while, Roberts worked as a model for the Click Modeling Agency, but she wasn't very successful. "Her weight was fine and she has an incredibly photogenic face," said one of the employees at Click. "But I don't think she really gave it her best shot. Her focus was to become an actress."

When Julia first moved to New York, she tried modeling. She soon discovered, however, that she enjoyed acting much more than modeling.

For the next year-and-a-half, Roberts auditioned for commercials, TV shows, and anything else she could find. She didn't get called back for a second audition very often, but she kept at it. One thing she never did find the time for was acting lessons. She admitted going to a few classes. Roberts wanted hands-on acting experience.

All this time, Roberts's brother Eric was making a name for himself as a successful actor. In 1986, Eric began to film *Blood Red*, a western thriller. Eric told Peter Masterson, the director of the film, about his talented sister Julia. "Eric said, 'I've got this sister. Is it okay if she *plays* my sister?' " said Masterson. "He just said she was good." On Eric's recommendation, Roberts was cast in the movie.

Blood Red opened in 1987 and, although it wasn't a hit, Roberts learned a lot about the making of a movie. She was glad to get the acting experience and has remained grateful to her brother.

"Eric has given me advice and, of course, my first movie role," said Roberts in a 1990 interview. "But the biggest help has just been watching him, how wonderful he is, and the choices he made."

Shortly before the making of *Blood Red*, Roberts and a friend were walking in New York when the friend ran into a casting agent she knew. The agent was immediately interested in Roberts. In early 1987, he helped her get a part on NBC-TV's popular series "Crime Story."

"Sometimes people seem kind of disappointed," said Roberts, "they want to hear about all these grueling years. But I'd never [looked for acting work] before. So I thought what I did must be pretty much what everyone does."

Despite her inexperience as an actor, acting offers began to come in after "Crime Story." Roberts's career was about to take off.

A BIG BREAK

After "Crime Story," Roberts was kept busy for the next year filming three movies. In each one, she had minor roles. But with each one, she gained recognition for her acting abilities.

In May 1987, she traveled to South Carolina to begin filming *Satisfaction*, a movie about four women in a rock and roll band. The teen comedy-drama starred Justine Bateman, another young actor, and was only a modest success.

While filming the movie, twenty-year-old Roberts fell in love with Liam Neeson, one of her costars. The two moved into a house in Venice, California, a few blocks from the ocean. The relationship didn't last long, however. A few weeks after finishing *Satisfaction*, Roberts left for Texas to film *Baja, California*, her third movie. Neeson stayed in California to pursue his own acting career.

In *Baja, California*, Roberts played the free-spirited daughter of Lesley Ann Warren. The movie was made for the HBO cable channel and was not praised by movie critics. Roberts, though, already had a contract for her next movie *Mystic Pizza*.

When she heard about the characters in *Mystic Pizza*, Roberts thought she was perfect for the role of the friend of Daisy, a beautiful waitress. She soon found out that the producers wanted her to play Daisy.

"I never considered myself a perfect beauty," confessed Roberts. She didn't think she was pretty enough for the part. So before her audition, Roberts spent "painstaking hours in the bathroom trying to look like this girl I went to high school with. She was stunning." The producers liked her audition and offered her the part of Daisy Araujo, a Portuguese pizza waitress who falls in love with a rich boy.

The filming took place in Mystic, Connecticut. Adam Stork, one of her costars, remembered how much fun Roberts was during filming. One day he heard laughter coming from one of the sets and went to investigate. "There was Julia," remembered Stork, "sitting on the steps of a house surrounded by about fifteen crew members. She had them eating out of her hand. They were just cracking up."

Roberts doesn't find it hard to be nice to people. "It is so easy to give affection to my family and friends," she said. "I get an instant response of a smile or something else. It just makes me feel good."

Mystic Pizza opened in 1988 and was a success. Critics praised Roberts's performance. Directors said that Julia Roberts was the star of the movie. Her portrayal of Daisy led to more important roles.

Roberts took time to consider what her next role should be. Through all the decision-making, she remained close to her mother and kept her informed of her growing career. "If I get a script I like," she explained, "I'll send it to my mother and ask her to read it. I want her to be involved with my life." A year after the success of *Mystic Pizza*, Roberts read the screenplay for *Steel Magnolias* and decided that she wanted a part in that movie.

STEEL MAGNOLIAS

Screenwriter Robert Harling had written a play about six Louisiana women who discuss their successes, disappointments, and joys in a beauty parlor. The play centered around the struggles of a mother with a diabetic daughter.

In the movie version, Roberts was cast as Shelby, the diabetic daughter of Sally Field. Dolly Parton, Shirley MacLaine, Daryl Hannah, and Olympia Dukakis were cast as the other main characters. As the newcomer to the screen, Roberts, at first, was unsure about working with such big stars.

"The first day it was a little shocking to be in the same room with all those [Academy Award-winning] women," confessed Roberts. "I wanted to take notes. But they were so down-to-earth. I felt I could go to them, and they helped me a lot."

Playing the part of Shelby required a lot of concentration. Roberts's character went from the joys of having a baby to the pain of kidney failure and eventually to death. "I didn't think I'd have the strength to play Shelby," said Roberts. "But I learned a lot of personal stuff on this movie."

Olympia Dukakis (left), Daryl Hannah, Julia, and Sally Field celebrate the success of their 1989 movie Steel Magnolias.

Roberts acted out her role as Shelby with a grueling method: She became so involved in her character that it was hard to let go after the filming was over. In one scene, said Robert Harling, Roberts "came as close to death as you can while you're still alive. After every take, they'd have to pick her up and help her back to her trailer. She would go all the way.

"I don't think [acting] lessons would have made much difference," Harling added. "She's just one of those people who's got it."

During the filming, Roberts began to date Dylan McDermott, the actor that played her on-screen husband in the movie. For a while the two were engaged to be married. But after a few months, the two called off the engagement.

Steel Magnolias debuted in November 1989. The movie clearly showed that Roberts was an extraordinary new acting talent. For her role, Roberts received her first Academy Award nomination as Best Supporting Actress. In an interview shortly after the announcement, Roberts said being nominated was the biggest thrill since making finalist in the Miss Panthera beauty contest at her high school. "It was that kind of a feeling of 'I can't believe they picked me,' " she said.

For her role in Steel Magnolias, *Julia won her first Golden Globe Award for Best Supporting Actress.*

Although she did not receive an Oscar from the Academy, she did win a Golden Globe Award for her performance. "I have to say the Golden Globes was the most shocking night of my life," said Roberts. "I was so unprepared."

Roberts realized that she owed much to the other actors in the film. "I learned so much from those women in *Steel Magnolias*," said Roberts. "I owe them a lot more than I could ever articulate. I just watched five tremendous women do what they do close to perfection."

MORE MOVIES AND MORE SUCCESS

Shortly before *Steel Magnolias* opened, Roberts had taken a fancy to a script about a prostitute and a ruthless businessman. The script was titled *Three Thousand*, after the prostitute's price for a week of work. Roberts auditioned for the part and won it.

The producers at Disney liked the idea but wanted a lighter, more humorous story. When the script was rewritten, it was renamed *Pretty Woman*.

The story was simple: Vivian, a good-hearted prostitute, meets Edward Lewis, a lonely hard-nosed businessman. As their relationship develops, Vivian slowly shows Edward that there is more to life than business deals and money-making.

Once Roberts saw the rewrite, she had to decide if she wanted to do the new movie. When she did, she had to audition for the part of Vivian all over again.

"I just loved [the character]," said Roberts. "My reaction to her was a balance of intrigue and fear–the same balance I felt toward Daisy in *Mystic Pizza* and Shelby in *Steel Magnolias*."

Once again, cast and crew members found it easy to like Roberts. "Julia has a magic up there on the screen," said Garry Marshall, the movie's director.

"I've worked with actresses who have been really difficult and she's not one of them," praised Richard Gere, her costar. "She's a very real and decent person, and she's not caught up in the actress thing."

When *Pretty Woman* opened in the summer of 1990, Roberts hardly had time to enjoy its success. She was already finishing up her next movie, *Flatliners*.

Julia costarred with Richard Gere in the 1990 hit comedy Pretty Woman.

The science-fiction thriller *Flatliners* costarred Roberts as one of a group of medical students who experiment with the boundary between life and death. The medical students induce brain death in each other, experience the fringes of death, and then are revived.

Once again the role required great concentration as Roberts's character "died," met her dead father, and then revived. Joel Schumacher, the film's director, was impressed with Roberts's performance. "Julia goes away and stays in character between takes until we get the scene done," he said. "She knows 'Action' isn't where the acting begins and 'Take' isn't always where it ends."

Where did Roberts learn to act so intensely? "I've worked with some really great actors," she explained, "and I hear them talking about structure, and I listen. But mostly, I watch."

The majority of the *Flatliners* scenes were shot around Christmas in 1989. At that time many of the crew members' children visited the set. "There was always a line of kids in and out of Julia's trailer," said Schumacher. "She was feeding them and mothering them."

Although she loves acting, Roberts admits that, one day, she wants to get married and have children. "There are times when I get so bogged down by the policies of this business that I just have these great domestic fantasies," she said. "Being at home, and being quiet, and reading, and having a garden, and doing all that stuff. Taking care of a family. Those are the most important things. Movies will come and go, but family is a real kind of consistency."

A NEW LOVE

During the filming of *Flatliners*, Roberts began dating one of her costars. But something about this relationship was different from all the others. "We're just real happy," said Roberts about her relationship with actor Kiefer Sutherland. "I've been lucky to find someone who I not only like and is my best friend but who I so admire and respect."

Kiefer also admires Roberts's many talents. "My initial attraction to Julia was to her incredible talent as an actor," he said. "And I adopted a phenomenal, ridiculous respect that evolved into something else."

Julia began to date actor Kiefer Sutherland while filming Flatliners. *The two became unofficially engaged in late 1990.*

"We're together all the time," added Roberts. "We work together, we're in love with each other. That's a life. You can't ask for more."

Kiefer visited her on the set of her next movie, *Sleeping With The Enemy*. The movie is about a woman married to a controlling, possessive husband. The woman escapes from him and builds a new life. But he eventually tracks her down.

"Whenever Kiefer would show up and spend time, Julia's mood would always get good," said Joseph Ruben, the movie's director. "I think they make each other laugh." In late 1990, Kiefer gave Roberts a ring and the two became unofficially engaged.

Also that year, Roberts bought a million-dollar house in Benedict Canyon in the Hollywood Hills of California. She has not had much time to enjoy her new home, however.

When the filming of *Sleeping With The Enemy* was completed, Roberts decided to take a break. She had been working steadily for the past year and had made three successful movies. Now she wanted to relax. During her break, she rarely went out except to attend an occasional Hollywood party. But she didn't rest all the time. She kept reading scripts and negotiating new contracts for herself.

In 1990, after making three successful movies, Julia decided to take a break before starting her next movie projects.

DEVOTED TO HER CRAFT

Five years had passed since her first movie. In 1991, Roberts was still determined to handle her career by taking things as they came. She remains devoted to her craft but knows that the acting business can be uncertain.

"Work does get you work," she explained. "Really, it's just a matter of luck and timing, getting that first momentum that can carry you somewhere, so you can show what you can do."

Her next film, *Dying Young*, debuted in the summer of 1991. Her role in this romantic movie was similar to her part in *Pretty Woman*. Roberts played a young nurse from a poor family who falls in love with a rich man dying from a deadly disease.

But Roberts didn't stop with that movie. *Hook*, directed by Steven Spielberg, came out in the winter of 1991. Robin Williams and Dustin Hoffman costarred in this updated version of Peter Pan in which Roberts played Tinkerbell.

1991 was another triumphant year for Julia; she worked on new movies and enjoyed her star status.

WHAT'S NEXT?

Roberts's movie career has been successful. Even her Georgia high school recognizes her acting talent. When Roberts was enrolled in Campbell High, the school didn't have any acting programs. Today, it offers many theater classes and awards a prize each year to the most promising acting student. The award is appropriately called the Julia Roberts Award.

What's in the future for this young actress? "I have goals, real simple things that are hard to attain," said Roberts. "I want to have a family, raise kids, be in love–all those things come way before work. My goals *there* are mainly to keep working."

Roberts remains optimistic about her future, despite the many changes that have taken place. In the summer of 1991, Roberts called off her engagement to Kiefer Sutherland and began to date other men. Julia Roberts knows that change is a part of growing and living. "Nothing lasts forever–not beauty, not a career," she cautioned herself. "Everything changes and gets better."

Julia has many goals for the future. She hopes to continue acting and to someday raise a family.

JULIA ROBERTS'S ADDRESS

You can write to Julia Roberts at:

Julia Roberts
c/o William Morris Agency
151 El Camino Drive
Beverly Hills, CA 90212